Lifted Out

My Journey to Freedom
From the Pit of Verbal and Emotional Abuse
To a Life of Grace and Redemption

CINDI MORSE

Lifted Out: My Journey to Freedom from the Pit of Verbal and Emotional Abuse to a Life of Grace and Redemption

Copyright © by Cindi Morse

All rights reserved. No part of this publication may be reproduced, distributed or transmitted in any form or by any means, including photocopying, recording, or other electronic or mechanical methods, without the prior written permission of the publisher, except in the case of brief quotations embodied in critical reviews and certain other noncommercial uses permitted by copyright law. For permission requests, write to the author at the email address below.

Cover design by Micah Rott
Editing/typesetting by Liz Smith of InkSmithEditing.com
Author photo by Regina Ochs with Flawless Faces & Photos

Unless otherwise noted, Scripture quotations are from the ESV® Bible (The Holy Bible, English Standard Version®), copyright © 2001 by Crossway, a publishing ministry of Good News Publishers. Used by permission. All rights reserved.

Scripture quotations marked (MSG) are taken from THE MESSAGE, copyright © 1993, 2002, 2018 by Eugene H. Peterson. Used by permission of NavPress. All rights reserved. Represented by Tyndale House Publishers, Inc.

Scripture quotations marked (NLT) are taken from the Holy Bible, New Living Translation, copyright ©1996, 2004, 2015 by Tyndale House Foundation. Used by permission of Tyndale House Publishers, Inc., Carol Stream, Illinois 60188. All rights reserved.

Scripture quotations marked CSB have been taken from the Christian Standard Bible®, Copyright © 2017 by Holman Bible Publishers. Used by permission. Christian Standard Bible® and CSB® are federally registered trademarks of Holman Bible Publishers.

Scripture quotations marked (NIV) are taken from the Holy Bible, New International Version®, NIV®. Copyright © 1973, 1978, 1984, 2011 by Biblica, Inc.™ Used by permission of Zondervan. All rights reserved worldwide. www.zondervan.com The "NIV" and "New International Version" are trademarks registered in the United States Patent and Trademark Office by Biblica, Inc.™

Scripture quotations marked (NRSV) are from New Revised Standard Version Bible, copyright © 1989 National Council of the Churches of Christ in the United States of America. Used by permission. All rights reserved worldwide.

Scripture quotations marked (GNT) are from the Good News Translation in Today's English Version- Second Edition Copyright © 1992 by American Bible Society. Used by Permission.

Lifted Out: My Journey to Freedom from the Pit of Verbal and Emotional Abuse to a Life of Grace and Redemption/Cindi Morse

ISBN: 978-0-578-57832-3

We are all on a journey, and within that journey, we each have a story. This is my story of pain and struggle, of defeat and despair, but also of strength and healing, of grace and redemption, of joy and hope. It isn't all pretty, and it wasn't at all easy, but God's grace is enough, His mercies are new every morning, and His faithfulness is great.

Contents

Acknowledgements vii
Foreword 1
Preface 7
Prologue 10
God's Plan Has Not Changed 13
Stronger Than I Thought I Was 35
God's Word Heals 47
My Posse 57
Our Furry Miracle 69
Oh, My Heart 79
It's All Jesus 89
About the Author 97

Acknowledgements

It is with deep gratitude that I say thank you to the people listed below. Each of you have walked this journey with me in some form or another, and you are all more precious to me than I can say. You have seen me at the bottom of the pit, and you didn't run. You stayed and prayed and listened and advised and loved. I am forever in your debt.

Mom—You taught me how to love and care for those around me, how to be a great mom and a faithful wife, and you taught me how to love Jesus. You have been a stellar example of His love and grace. Thank you.

Daddy—Thank you for sharing your wisdom with me. God has rewarded your faithfulness to Him in so many ways, and I am beyond blessed to have benefitted from

Acknowledgements

those rewards. Your kind and gentle way of living in grace toward those around you is truly a rare thing to behold, and I am grateful to have known you my whole life.

Kristi—My dear sister, I'm so happy we are close friends. Thank you for always loving me and my boys with such a generous spirit. You are a treasure.

Micah Rott—The best BFF a girl could have. Thank you for always listening, always encouraging, and always believing. I truly would not have made it out without you. I will always treasure those years we lived close enough to walk together, as well as your patience and willingness to hear my heart and the sacrifice of your time and sanity to accompany me in watching hours of Hallmark movies. You're a rock star.

Lisa Bozarth—Thank you for reading my manuscript and for offering such excellent advice and wisdom throughout my writing. You are so much more than my web designer, though you have certainly surpassed my expectations in that arena as well.

Cathy, Barb, and Delinda—a.k.a. my Zoom girls. You are, without a doubt, the push and encouragement I needed to step out of my comfort zone and embrace all that God has for me, both personally and professionally. "Thank you" is not enough.

Pastor Nathan and Pastor Reid—I am so grateful for the truth that you so unwaveringly share with us each week. God's truth is not always what we want to hear, but it is always what we need to hear. Thank you for serving Him so valiantly and for leading us so well.

And finally, to the loves of my life:

Don—You are the man God made for me to spend life with, the husband I have always dreamed of, and an amazing example of Christlike love for my boys to see. There will never be enough time for us on this earth, but I will love you with everything I have for as long as God gives us. You are my sweet true love, the best there could ever be, and I am so blessed and grateful that God brought us together. I am more in love with you every day. Forever and always, my love.

Acknowledgements

Jackson, Dawson, and Roman—I have loved you and dreamed about you since I discovered baby dolls as a child. You are far and away more than I ever could have asked for. You have been my life's purpose and my heart's passion for as long as I can remember, and my "Mama heart" grows with pride and love for each of you with every breath.

Drew, Adrianna, and Sydney—my Bonus Brood. We got a late start on this family thing, but I am so grateful for each of you every day. Thank you for accepting my boys and me so easily and respectfully, for including us in your family. I love you all.

Foreword

I am a pastor. The Bible is my ultimate authority, so it's no trouble for me to say, "God hates divorce." I know that, I preach that, and I fervently long for and work toward forgiveness and reconciliation in every situation. In my line of work, this consumes a good portion of my time, and I don't believe that anyone should ever consider divorce lightly.

Yet, what I missed in my early years of pastoral ministry, and what I believe so many pastors and others tend to miss today, is that God also hates abuse, including emotional abuse. I'm not sure there are many things God hates more than abuse. If you were to add up all the commands about destructive words, degrading oppression, damaging anger, and despicable violence, you would certainly see how near this subject is to the heart of God.

Foreword

When those things appear in a marriage, it must break His heart. Marriage is meant to be God's living metaphor to the world. God is our Husband, and He loves us with self-sacrifice, forgiveness, patience, goodness and righteousness. He will never abuse or betray, leave us, or divorce us. When a marriage continues in opposition to this design, it shows us a false version of God's love. An abusing spouse is actually telling lies about God. To his wife. To his kids. To the watching world.

And this abuse is everywhere. Even in my church. It's in your church too. Your community, your neighborhood, and among your coworkers. You are not alone.

I was so naive when I became a pastor. Sure, there are abusive marriages "out there somewhere," but surely, none of the families I know. I didn't even have a category for the difference between a disappointing marriage (for which there is no biblical grounds for divorce) and a destructive marriage (for which there may be biblical grounds for divorce and certainly for separation).

Walking with Cindi has helped me see the difference. I've been Cindi's pastor since 2006. Reading this book brought back plenty of my own memories of how she and I talked and prayed and cried together over the years. What my friend Cindi and others like her have helped me see is three things in particular.

First, she has helped me see the difference between a disappointing marriage and a destructive one. These are not the same thing, and if you are wrestling to discern which marriage you have, you need to read this book, and you also need to spend time with godly friends, mentors, pastors, and therapists to discern your situation.

You need a church, and not just one who will tell you what you want to hear but one who approaches these matters with both truth and grace. Only when you diagnose the problem can you begin working on the solution. If you are considering divorce, you must take this step first, and with community.

Foreword

Second, Cindi has taught me how to suffer with faithfulness. It'll only take you a couple of hours to read this book. Keep in mind it took years for Cindi to live it. There are no quick fixes here, and she's honest about that.

It was never easy for Cindi or her boys. Yet she stayed close to Jesus, and the habits you'll see in this book played an essential role in that. If you want your faith to survive (and even thrive), the things she does, like church community, prayer, Scripture meditation, and meaningful friendships are not just good storytelling, they're necessary for your soul. They kept her alive, and she did them even when she didn't feel like it.

And third, Cindi has shown me that God can redeem and restore even the ugliest messes—not necessarily how she or I originally prayed but in His own way.

And listen, this is really important. The happy ending in this story is not her marriage to Don. No disrespect to Don—Don is a good man. It was a delight performing their marriage ceremony, uniting their families. As Cindi says, I got a front-row seat to

God's redemption in their story, and I praise God for that.

But that's not the real happy ending, and you cannot expect your story to end the same. God may have different plans for you, and the road ahead may be much longer. The happy ending here is a woman who has stayed faithful to God, found joy amid heartache, and waited for Jesus to show up. And He did.

And He will for you too. It may not look like what you want, and the path before you may still be long and ragged, but God is for you. And if you are with Him, through Jesus, He will make it right—whatever it is. With Him, you too can find joy.

Pastor Nathan Miller, Christ Community Evangelical Free Church

Preface

Dear Friend,

I am so humbled and grateful that you have picked up this book. I want you to know that I have been thinking of you and praying for you for years. You have inspired me to continue this journey. You have been the heart behind my determination to write my story. You are the reason I have walked this path with strength and grace—so that I could pass along to you what I have learned.

I love this path that God has ordained for me. It has been wonderful, harsh, painful, amazing, and at times, more than I could bear on my own. But God. But God has always been with me, as promised in 2 Corinthians 1:3-5 which says, "Praise be to the God and Father of our Lord Jesus Christ, the Father of compassion and the God of all comfort, who comforts us in all our troubles, so that we can

Preface

comfort those in any trouble with the comfort we ourselves receive from God. For just as we share abundantly in the sufferings of Christ, so also our comfort abounds through Christ." He has sustained me, provided for me, and held me up so I could tell you my story so He could bring hope to your heart.

I could tell you every sordid detail, every painful, ugly, contemptuous taunt that was hurled in my direction and that of my children; I could replay hundreds of sleepless and emotionally tortured nights, but that is not what this book is about. Those things happened, to be sure, but the focus of this book—the reason for my efforts of putting pen to paper—is to show the grace and redemption of Christ, to uplift and encourage women who are where I was that God is good and He is able. He sees you where you are, and He loves you. I am living proof that He is able to do exceedingly abundantly more than we can ask or think (Eph. 3:20) when we trust and follow Him.

I want you to know that you did not pick up this book by accident. If someone recommended it, I am truly humbled. If you "happened upon it," I am sincerely grateful, but either way, it is not an accident. God has led you here on purpose. He has something in my story that you need to hear. It is His gift to you, proof that He loves you. It is evidence of His mercy toward you.

Thank you in advance, for reading and for walking with me through the pages of this story, this path that God has divinely placed me on, for just such a time as this. May you feel His love, His presence, His mercy, and His passion for you as you read. I hope to meet you someday, to look in your eyes, to hear your story of God's grace and redemption in your life, and to rejoice with you.

By His grace alone,

Cindi

Prologue

Demoralized and tossed aside, I was trapped in a deep dark pit, clawing desperately through what felt like barbed wire, my hands and my heart raw and bloody, my face streaked with dirt and tears, my mind swirling with fear and panic, as I felt his foot placed firmly on top of my head, pushing me deeper and deeper into the abyss with every hateful word. *You're not enough. You're so stupid. You're not good at anything. You're so disgusting. You're too fat to be loved. Why would anyone ever be attracted to you?*

The disconsolate cry of my heart reverberated in my head with every heartbeat: *This can't be my life. I was made for more than this. GOD, PLEASE GET ME OUT OF HERE!!! I can't take this anymore!*

This was the recurring nightmare I awoke to every day for far longer than I care to admit. I did not dig the metaphorical pit. I did not climb into it. But I allowed it to be dug. I allowed him to sling those verbal assaults at me day after day and year after year, and I stayed, giving him unspoken permission to continue the verbal and emotional oppression that became the hallmark of our daily lives.

This is my story. It is one of painful emotional, verbal, and psychological abuse. More importantly, it is a story of how God lifted me out of that pit of despair, raised me up in His grace, and redeemed my heart and life.

— 1 —

God's Plan Has Not Changed

> *I know what I'm doing. I have it all planned out—plans to take care of you, not abandon you, plans to give you the future you hope for.*
> *– Jeremiah 29:11 (MSG)*

Have you ever done something—or had something happen to you—that convinced you that God's plan for your life was ruined? I have. Many times, actually. I've done stupid things in high school or college and in my twenties (and thirties and forties), and I'd think, "Well, I just screwed that up. No way God's perfect plan for me will work now." But the time I felt it the most intensely was when my husband of seventeen years told me he was leaving. Truthfully, I should have seen it coming. It had been brewing for most of our marriage. Nevertheless, my heart was somehow T-boned as he told me he was leaving, that he saw no future with me in it, that he had developed a deep hatred for me and had absolutely no interest in counseling or any attempt in working things out.

We had met eighteen years earlier while in a large young adult singles Bible study. He was a small group leader with a heart for Jesus, and I was attending my first study since moving back home from a job several hundred miles away. We hit it off at a gathering of a few of the small groups. With about four hundred young adult singles in the study, several groups would get together at smaller mixers to facilitate more meaningful connections. One such mixer was at the house where he lived with three other guys. We didn't get many chances to talk that night, but interests were piqued, and we made more of a point to notice each other at the study over the next few weeks. Several of us would grab something to eat after the study each week and sit around the table and talk and laugh, and so he and I began to get to know each other. When we started dating, it was very lighthearted and fun. We truly enjoyed being together, and I remember laughing as we played mini golf, went to movies, and did other dating-type activities. We got to be close friends with two other dating couples from the study and enjoyed time having cookouts and going out with them as well.

We got engaged about six months after we started dating and married six or seven months later.

We were twenty-eight and twenty-nine when we married and figured we were old enough to know what we wanted and when we'd found it. I knew he had some insecurities with relationships and was concerned about marriage, as he "didn't want a marriage like his parents had." I remember him telling me that his dog had really been the one to teach him about loyalty and unconditional love, which I thought was horribly sad, but I—of course—thought I could be the one to show him what love and loyalty looked like from a human perspective and he would obviously respond in a perfectly reciprocal way. I know. I literally cannot roll my eyes back into my head far enough. So many things in our lives are painfully obvious in hindsight, yet we are completely incapable of seeing those things at the time.

In the beginning, we spent many evenings with my parents playing cards. We typically played Hand and Foot but would sometimes switch it up and play Rook. We really went all out, right?! My mom would cook dinner, and after we ate we would clear the table and get the games started. Most of the time we played guys against girls. Sometimes we got a bit feisty and competitive with each other, but we were always able to laugh and end on a good note. So far, so good.

Unfortunately, we were married only a few months when things began happening that should have been a pretty big clue as to what the future would hold.

The first time I can recall being scared of him was probably six months into our marriage, during a fight about money. He would lay all the bills out on the counter in the kitchen—not in a stack but unfolded and laid out, taking up a space of maybe a foot by two feet or so—and that's where they would stay. One day as I was cleaning, I stacked the bills so I could easily pick them up and wipe the counter, and then left them right on the counter where they had been—but in a stack so they didn't take up as much space. Several days later, he went through them and realized one of the bills had been due a day or two before. By his reaction, you would have thought I had shredded a thousand dollars. He ranted and raved, threw things around the apartment, and screamed insults at me. He blamed me for messing up his system and said we would never be able to buy a home or a car because I had ruined his perfect credit. (Looking back, I should probably have run as far as I could, but again, hindsight is 20/20, and I was brought up to believe that marriage is forever and divorce was never to be mentioned or considered as an option—and I took that very seriously.)

In retrospect though, that was the beginning of what would, over the next seventeen years, become a daily nightmare of insults and degradations about my intelligence (or my *stupidity*, as he would say), my talents and abilities (of which he said I had none), and my weight (beginning with my first of four pregnancies, three of which were carried to full term and resulted in three beautiful boys who are my most loved and prized gifts from heaven).

A couple times in the first two or three years he would clear his desk in one angry swipe. Three times I remember him being so angry that he stood in front of me, grabbed the arms of the chair I was sitting in, and shook the chair—and me with it—as hard as he could. He's one of those men who looks intimidating anyway, and with angry daggers shooting out of his eyes, it's just downright terrifying. (I realized later that, for me, the appeal of his intimidating looks was that he would scare others away and I would be protected. Unfortunately, I also learned that he is not a protector, and what early on I had thought was protectiveness was apparently all an act.)

The one constant I could pretty much count on was the yelling. He grew up in a home that whoever yelled the loudest won the argument, so he'd had plenty of practice, whereas in my home we would talk things out calmly (not that voices were never raised, but we certainly didn't berate each other or walk away feeling as if we had been verbally assaulted). I didn't stand a chance in the verbal ring with him.

One vivid memory of this was in our second apartment. We'd been married a little over a year, and I don't remember what set him off, but he was furious. He stood over me yelling and cursing and pointing in my face, while I sat quietly on the couch trying to figure out what had triggered his anger and how to get away from his tirade.

Finally, he paused his rant and stepped a few feet away. Jumping at the opportunity, I got up and began to walk toward the bedroom. As I hurried down the hall, he turned and told me, with disgust dripping from his words, that I was weak and had no backbone because I wouldn't even fight with him. I later told him that it takes more backbone than he would ever know to sit there quietly while he hurled such hate-filled words at me, but at that moment, I was speechless, and continued my way down the hall in silence. In the bedroom, I lay down on the bed, sobbing, overcome with emotional pain and confusion. *What was happening here?*

That day I asked myself a telltale question that I would ask repeatedly over nearly two decades more: What did *I* do to make him act like that? It took me seventeen years and a lot of therapy to be able to answer that question I asked so many times: I didn't do anything to make him act like that; it's not about me, it's about him.

As is usually the case, it began with one incident, but over the years it became an everyday occurrence that shaped and molded our home. Misery became the emotion my boys and I identified with daily, almost without exception.

I should pause here a moment and admit something. Over time, I developed a sizable protective and deflective shield to help me combat the arrows of his words. You see, God made me feisty. I've always known it, have often been criticized for it, and for most of my life, I felt like it was something to be ashamed of, something I needed to conquer. But I honestly believe that spunk was what kept me from being swallowed up all those years. It kept me going, strengthened my resolve, and gave me the chutzpah I needed to survive. I am so grateful for my feisty spirit now.

I am still working on tempering that toughness a bit, as it also tends to lean toward unnecessary and overzealous defensiveness at times, but God knew I would need that gumption to survive. Many times my self-defense was unkind and my words were hurtful, but I also know I would feel horrible about the things I had said, and I would apologize (probably not without exception but pretty darn close). Granted, my apologies were met with responses of "I don't need your apologies" and "Whatever" (oooooh, I still hate that word), but I wanted to honor God to the best of my ability, so I continued to apologize when I lost the battle to control my tongue. It is because of Jesus that I was able to survive and keep hold of the faith that He gave me. It is because of Jesus that I was able to fight back for myself, my children, and the life that God created me for and redeemed for me.

Shortly before our third son was born, about nine years in, he began sleeping on the living room floor on the weekends, which then became most nights, and then every night the last four or five years. He would fall asleep watching television on the floor or, sometimes, the couch and would remain there until morning. I would get up to wake the boys for school, and he would go shower and get ready for work. Most mornings we didn't speak at all, a welcome recess from the yelling, though it was horribly awkward on its own.

A few months before the separation, he adopted an agonizing habit of spewing vicious, venomous words at me before turning and striding out the door, slamming it as he bailed from the chaos he had just created, to go to work most every morning. I would be in the kitchen making lunches for our boys and would end up in tears, fighting to stay on my feet until my oldest, who was thirteen at the time, could run in and hold me up as I collapsed in his sweet, young arms. He would say to me, "Mom, don't listen to him. He's wrong, Mom. He doesn't know you at all. He has no idea who you are. Don't listen to his lies. He's just a jackass." My mid-kid, eleven, would come in and join the hug and give credence to his brother's words while simultaneously trying to protect his seven-year-old brother from the heartbreaking scene. My boys were my lifeline, and their words were salve to my wounded heart, but it nearly broke me that they had to hear those things from the man who had promised to be a godly husband and father and the spiritual leader of our home. How far he had fallen from that Bible study leader from eighteen years earlier.

This is what life was like when I began seeing a counselor on my own, for the third time in our marriage, as he again refused to join me. After a couple of sessions where I would describe the current condition of our relationship, the counselor informed me that what I was describing was domestic abuse. I have never thought of myself as a victim and had certainly never put the label of "abuse" on what I was living with, but when she explained it, and as I began to read more about verbal and emotional abuse, it all became clear.

I remember the day I made the decision to have the conversation with him, stating in no uncertain terms that things were about to change. My counselor and I had been discussing the lifelong belief that had been instilled in me that divorce was never an option. No matter what, you stick it out and make it work.

What was never discussed in my church or in my home was the *reason* God hates divorce. He doesn't hate the people involved, but He does hate the pain and destruction that leads to the choice or need to divorce and the ensuing wreckage that is left in its wake. The family is His prized creation, and the destruction of it always damages those who are affected by it, sometimes badly crippling those entangled in its snare. This is what God hates.

My counselor and I continued to discuss the current situation; she listened and then gave me the bottom-line assessment. She said that I had been trying so hard to keep my marriage together all by myself—to keep the train on the tracks, so to speak—and I had failed to realize that the train was not only off the track but had skidded out of control to the bottom of the hill and was lying on its side. She explained that the decision now was not about keeping the train on the track but whether I would choose to sit in it till it blew up or get up, grab my kids, and get out. I don't think I will ever forget that visual or the heart-stopping impact as it hit me between the eyes. I had a choice. *Finally*, someone told me that *I* had a choice.

I made a decision that day. I could go on living this way, more miserable with each passing day, fear coursing through me and my boys every time the garage door went up, as we braced ourselves wondering what mood he would be in when he walked through the door. But I chose not to. There was *no way* I was going to continue to subject my kids and myself to the damage and indignities we had been living with.

I began to pray daily about the timing of this inevitable verbal exchange, and it was five or six weeks before I would feel God's peace about having the conversation that would change everything. I was washing dishes after dinner one evening, mulling over the most recent verbal venom that he had so carelessly spit in my direction as he escaped, as usual, to the living room to watch television. A palpable wave of peace and God's presence began to envelope me. I felt His gentle nudging, indicating the time had come. I walked calmly into the living room, my head held high with the confidence only Christ can give, asked for his full attention, and told him I was done. I would no longer live this way. I would no longer hold myself and our children hostage to his emotional and verbal abuse. And I gave him a choice: either agree and commit to going to marriage counseling with me until we could make our home a healthy place for us and our boys, or he needed to go. It was his choice, but those were his only options.

His decision came less than two weeks later, the night that the life I knew crumbled and my journey to freedom began, the journey and the freedom that God had prepared for me all along.

It was after midnight when he finally left that night, but I was reeling. It's almost funny to me now that I was so shocked. All the signs that the marriage was over had been there for a long time, but somehow, I thought that the idea of divorce would wake him and shake him and God would miraculously heal everything, making us into a family with a great story of God's redemption and healing. It honestly never occurred to me that he would walk away. He did, however, and so after he left, I called my mom. We talked and cried for a while, rehashing the entire conversation of the night. She cried with me and tried to encourage me that everything would be okay. Finally, she prayed with me before I fell exhausted into bed.

I remember thinking, *This is not how my life was supposed to go. This was NOT God's perfect plan for me and my boys*, as I drifted off to sleep. The next morning, I realized I had slept more soundly, deeply, peacefully, and fearlessly than I had in more years than I could remember. I awoke feeling both devastated and relieved—devastated because the dream I'd had all those years earlier had been destroyed, along with my self-worth and that of my children, and relieved because I was securely wrapped in the peace of God that truly passes all understanding, and *He* would *never* leave us.

It's funny how God works sometimes. What I feared the most—divorce—became the thing that set me free. I didn't even realize how afraid I was until he was no longer there, but as I spent time alone in that big house, a single mom of three boys, I was fully shrouded in the most beautiful blanket of peace I had ever known, and I became more acutely aware of that peace every day.

Now, don't get me wrong, I had some bad days—some *really bad* days—but even in the midst of the pain of his rejection and infidelity (which I found out about a few weeks into the separation, a punch to the gut that sent me reeling in ways I never could have imagined), an underlying peace pulled me through. While it was easily the deepest, rawest pain that my boys and I had ever felt, and we battled through a lot of hurt and rejection and wrestled with a lot of questions, we grounded our hope in Christ and in His promises: *He* would never leave us nor forsake us, *He* would always love us, *He* would always be faithful, and *His* plan for us was still for good.

It was a long journey, and I learned so much about God during that time. As a point of background, we had been faithfully attending the same church as a family for about sixteen years. Through that church, we were involved in a small group with four other families who met weekly when the boys were in early elementary school; we went through a couples Bible study class at our church after that, and I had been involved in several women's Bible studies ever since. Even though he was still attending church with us, I could tell it had stopped being important or interesting to him. He had not made the effort to attend a men's study for at least six years and had never led any type of study or devotions with our kids at home, leaving the spiritual teaching to me (which wasn't something he wanted me to do either).

Because I had grown up in a home where we talked about God and had devotions often, I knew how important it was for the boys to have it be a regular part of our everyday discussions, and I have always taken my responsibility to teach my boys very seriously. When their dad moved out, I felt that same responsibility, though heightened—as well as a new freedom to dig in deeper to who God is and what that means for each of us in our daily lives—so my boys and I immediately began having a devotion together every night. I wanted them to learn, above everything else, that Jesus is still good and that He is the one we run to *always*.

So we gathered together every night to read a devotion and some Bible verses and to pray. We prayed for their dad, and we prayed for each other and the different ways we were all struggling to make sense of it. And God showed up, as He always does, and He taught us so much. He taught us that His plan from the beginning of time included this heart-wrenching period in our lives and that although we didn't see it coming, He did. This wasn't something that came out of nowhere or something that God had to suddenly work around or squeeze into His already full plan for us. He knew this would happen, and He intended to work it for our good. Nothing surprises our Savior. Nothing. Things shock the heck out of me occasionally, but He is never surprised.

When I realized that He had figured this into our life story before we were even born, it took my breath away. In fact, in no way could I truly fulfill His plan for me *without* going through the divorce or the verbal and emotional abuse I endured. Without those things, I wouldn't be writing this book today, you wouldn't be reading it, and I wouldn't be connecting with women who need my story of God's grace and redemption.

We often don't want to think of the hard and painful things as part of His plan, but without those things, we would never be so empty and so desperate for a Savior that we fall on our faces and give Him everything. It's through the pain and agony that I've learned the most about Him. It's scary to lose our way and mind-boggling and heartrending to have the life we know thrown into a lidless blender, then have that blender flipped on, tossing the pieces in a million directions. But God is there, and He says, "Yep, I planned for this too. Just wait to see the beauty I have in store for you. *Trust me with this.*"

And so we did, and we are better for it.

During the two years that it took for the divorce to finalize, I pressed into Jesus and relied on Him, my counselor, my family and friends, and the stories of other women—women who had been there before me, who had not only survived but were now blossoming into the beautiful, confident women God created them to be, who had found hope in the midst of their darkest, most excruciating moments and had come out on the other side full of joy and hope. Oh, how I wanted that hope! I felt like a dried-up loofah trying to soak it all in, yet it felt as if most of it just ran through the holes in my heart. But I got up every day and drenched myself in God's Word and in those beautiful stories of God's grace and redemption, and eventually my heart was able to heal, and I, too, came out on the other side of my darkest days full of joy and hope.

It was in and through that experience that God put a fire in my soul. He had placed me on a path that would be painful and hard, and He knew I would collapse in His lap and let Him be my strength. He knew my divorce would take two years. He knew that was exactly how long my therapy would take, how long it would take for me to get to the point of being able to rejoice in that courtroom rather than fall apart, to walk out in strength with my head held high rather than the shattered mess I had been months before. He knew the people whose stories gave me hope as they were walking through their pain. He knew I would need each story.

> *God knows the path you have walked. He knows the hurt, and He knows the strength you have found, or need to find, in Him. And He knows who needs your story. He knows the lives you will touch, the beauty that will come from the ashes, and the hearts that will be healed as they are opened to Him and His perfect love, grace, and redemption. If you're still in the middle of your story, take heart. You can trust Him. He is faithful. He has good ahead for you, plans to give you the future you hope for.*

— 2 —

Stronger Than I Thought I Was

Always remember:

*You are BRAVER than you believe,
STRONGER than you seem,
SMARTER than you think, and
Twice as BEAUTIFUL as you've ever imagined.*

I have always loved that quote. I don't know that it's ever been credited to any particular person, but I think it truly reflects the heart of God for each of us. I think I always knew deep down—even when I was too afraid to believe anything good about myself—that I am strong and brave. That's a strange concept to me now. *I was afraid to believe anything good about myself.* Why, you ask? What if I was wrong? More importantly, what if *he* was right? After all, he kept telling me how much smarter he was than I am, and maybe he really did know me best. Maybe I really was too stupid to have a conversation with. Maybe I really didn't have any talents or abilities. Maybe I really was unlovable.

Words are powerful. Words break people—not our bones but our spirits, which is far worse. We've all had people say unkind things about us—the girl at school who has everything but the courtesy to be nice to those who don't, the neighborhood bully who gains pleasure when others are notably affected by his or her stinging words; the list is endless—but hateful and destructive verbal arrows from those who have promised to love, honor, cherish, and protect us are much more damaging. Those arrows have teeth. They grip us at the deepest part of ourselves and chew a ragged hole that festers and twists with each repeated offense. They attack the heart and soul of who we are and leave us intensely wounded, utterly broken, hopelessly rejected, frightfully abandoned and desperately empty, until we either break completely or fight back.

Sometimes we do both.

Many of those arrows were maliciously and skillfully shot at me during that seventeen years of marriage, and during the two years of separation before the divorce was final, they gained in intensity as if they were lit on fire. Like the grand finale in a firework show, it was as if he knew the time was coming when he would no longer have the opportunity to ravage me with his words, so he hurled everything he had at the end. Had it not been for my boys, my church, my family, and my Jesus, I would surely have been devastated beyond recognition and would never have had the gumption to fight back.

But I did. I did fight back, with everything I had and then some. I fought back for my boys. I fought back for myself—my mental health, my self-respect, my future. I fought back because I refused to be destroyed, to be permanently manipulated out of who I was meant to be. I fought back because I want my boys to know how to fight back against the pressures around them that would try to manipulate their minds and change the direction of their souls. My boys are worth fighting for. I am worth fighting for.

I crawled into the arms of Jesus and allowed Him to be my comfort, strength, wisdom, and provider. Second Corinthians 1:8–9 says, "We do not want you to be uninformed . . . about the troubles we experienced. . . . We were under great pressure, far beyond our ability to endure, so that we despaired of life itself. . . . But this happened that we might not rely on ourselves but on God, who raises the dead." I collapsed in the lap of my Savior, and I relied on Him for everything that we needed. I can tell you that He provided more than I asked, more than I could have even dreamed of, through His Word, in my quiet times with Him and through the prayers and encouragement of friends and family, the stories of other Christian women who had seen His faithfulness in their struggles, and many Christian song artists as they shared their journeys through music.

Nevertheless, while we were finding our joy, it was challenged by the reality of our day-to-day existence. Bills needed to be paid, and all the normal things of a busy household—laundry, cooking, cleaning, errands, practices and games, school, and work—were still there. Somehow, I had to find the time and strength to do all those things while also dealing with the crushing blow of rejection and abandonment that replaced the fear. My boys were dealing with an enormous loss too, one that they did not understand or expect. All we knew was that our lives were forever changed and marked by this event and that, quite frankly, it sucked.

Every morning, I got up, got my kids dressed and fed and off to school, and I sat. I sat, heart and soul bared, on my couch with my Bible open and my journal and pen in hand. I prayed and cried and wrote and cried and prayed some more, until work and motherhood responsibilities could be delayed no longer.

I must pause here to tell you that I have the most amazing boys on the planet. I know that every parent thinks that, but these precious boys, who were hurting so badly themselves, feeling rejected, hurt, and confused, lovingly and compassionately hugged, loved, and literally and figuratively held me up. They have always been very protective of their beloved mama.

From the beginning, we had family devotions every night—we prayed together, read God's Word, shared, and encouraged one another. We grew closer every day. We bonded over God's Word and frozen pizza and shared laughter and tacos and *Castle* reruns. We had ups and downs, and some days were almost unbearable, but we came out with a stronger faith and a deeper appreciation for God and for His divine provision than we'd ever had, along with a strong desire for peace, calm, and gentleness.

Within a few weeks of the separation, I'd had an epiphany of sorts, as I realized that there was no way I could figure out my emotional trauma and help the boys navigate theirs at the same time. I simply didn't have the tools. So, I got a recommendation from my church, and we all went weekly to see a family counselor at our local Christian university. The interns get to see patients (with a supervisor keeping a close eye on the process) which helps ease them into their own practice, and the university offers the service at a discounted rate, an incredible blessing for a new single parent with three kiddos in immediate need. The boys and I had family sessions, then each of us went to one-on-one sessions so we could have a space to deal with our emotions and questions without feeling any familial pressure.

No matter how hard we fight or how determined we are, some things we cannot do alone. We weren't meant to. God created us to need others, and solid Christian counselors and therapists are among His most gracious gifts. I cannot even put into words how much we have benefitted from this. We have each learned that there are people you can trust. We've discovered the truth about *who* we are and *whose* we are.

We have learned it is not weakness but strength to ask for help, to recognize when we are overwhelmed or unable to make sense of our circumstances or when we are hurting too much to be able to see a way through it. We've been taught the ability to distinguish the truth about ourselves from the lies we were told. We've also realized you cannot change other people; we must accept who they are and take what they say accordingly. Maybe most importantly, we've learned that we are both lovable and deeply loved by so many. There have been many other lessons and strategies gained from these sessions as well, and I highly recommend this goldmine of God's abundant blessing.

Even now, I am so grateful my boys have a healthy view of good counseling and the benefit of it. They are not afraid to admit that they need to hash some stuff out with someone or that they need support from an unbiased, legally-required-to-keep-a-secret individual.

We continued to attend church. Every week. Whether we felt like it or not. When my boys began spending every other weekend with their dad, it was non-negotiable that they would be back on Sunday morning in time to get to church. It's who we are; it's what we do. It was our lifeline. The youth group, the Sunday school class, the community group, the friends, the pastors—all were inextricably linked to our getting through the divorce.

There are still hurts that we battle, words that trigger defense mechanisms, and scars that threaten to burst open, but we've come a long way, baby, and God is not finished with us yet. Even as I write my story, tears are running down my cheeks as I recall and relive not only the pain but also the deep and profound ways God has shown Himself to me, truly bringing me His indescribable joy. Paul says in 1 Peter 5:9–11 (MSG), "So keep a firm grip on the faith. The suffering won't last forever. It won't be long before this generous God who has great plans for us in Christ—eternal and glorious plans they are!—will have you put together and on your feet for good. He gets the last word; yes, he does." I LOVE that!! I love the Message translation, "put together and on your feet for good." YES!! This means YOU!! Go ahead, now, do that happy dance in exuberant expectation of what He is doing for *your* good. I'm right here dancing with you.

How are you fighting today? Are you sinking yourself into God's truth through His Word? Are you surrounding yourself with believers who will come beside you to be the strength and comfort you need? Have you researched the counseling options that are available to you? Are you capitalizing on those options? In what ways are you moving forward?

I cannot stress enough the importance of action in moving into your new freedom. God has great things ahead for you, and I don't want you to miss a single thing! According to James 1:5–6, "If any of you lacks wisdom, let him ask God, who gives generously to all without reproach, and it will be given him. But let him ask in faith, with no doubting." If you are unsure where to turn or how to move forward, ask for wisdom. God wants to talk to you. He wants to give you His direction for your life. Believe that He knows and loves you and wants to share His best with you. Ask Him to direct you with His wisdom, then trust that He will. You can do this with God's help. You are stronger than you think you are.

— 3 —

God's Word Heals

*As soon as I pray, you answer me;
 you encourage me by giving me strength. . . .
Though I am surrounded by troubles,
 you will protect me from the anger of my
  enemies.
You reach out your hand,
 and the power of your right hand saves me.
The Lord will work out his plans for my life—
 for your faithful love, O Lord, endures forever.
  – Psalm 138:3, 7–8 (NLT)*

> *I called on your name, O LORD,*
> *from the depths of the pit;*
> *You heard my plea, "Do not close*
> *your ear to my cry for help!"*
> *You came near when I called on you;*
> *You said, "Do not fear!"*
> *You have taken up my cause, O LORD;*
> *you have redeemed my life.*
> *– Lamentations 3:55–58*

I clung to these verses like a lifeline.

I would bet that you have some of those verses too, verses that are burned into your soul because of the impact they have had on you.

One day shortly after the separation, a dear friend sent me a card. In it she had written a prayer and some encouraging words. Along with that, she had enclosed several index cards with Scriptures written on them as well as a few blank cards for me to write some of my own. Her advice was that I place the cards all over the house where I would see them often and pray them back to God. I taped some to my kitchen window where I would see them as I washed dishes, and each time I stood there washing, I read those verses and talked to Jesus. I tucked a couple of cards into the corners of my bathroom mirror and prayed as I washed my face and got ready for my day. Those verses set the tone for my day, calmed me before I went to sleep, and encouraged me to keep going during the day when I was struggling to keep my head up.

I could fill several pages with precious verses from God's Word that brought me joy, peace, comfort and hope, but there are a few I feel God is gently tugging on my heart to share with you.

Let's start with the two at the beginning of the chapter:

> As soon as I pray, you answer me; you encourage me by giving me strength. Though I am surrounded by troubles, you will protect me from the anger of my enemies.
>
> You reach out your hand, and the power of your right hand saves me.

> The Lord will work out his plans for my life—for your faithful love, O Lord, endures forever.
>
> – Psalm 138:3, 7–8 (NLT)

> I called on your name, O LORD, from the depths of the pit;
>
> You heard my plea, "Do not close your ear to my cry for help!"
>
> You came near when I called on you;
>
> You said, "Do not fear!"
>
> You have taken up my cause, O LORD; you have redeemed my life.
>
> – Lamentations 3:55–58

We should take note of some similarities. *I* must call on *Him*. He is right there, but He's not pushy. He's not just going to jump in and take the pain away as we go about our lives. *We have to ask!* He will answer, but He waits for us to take the first step.

The next thing I notice in the pattern is "You encourage me by giving me strength" and "You came near." When we call out to Him, it's His turn to act. It's a dance of sorts. We move with Him, and He moves with us, but both of us are taking steps. No one is just standing there while the other dances around. It takes two; me and Jesus, you and Jesus. Put your arms around His neck, pull in close, lay your head on his chest, and dance. Oh, the comfort He brings when we relax and rest on Him.

When we rest, we find that He fights for us—and He wins! *He delivers us and takes up our cause.* Now, I know we always want this to look like God instantly slays the giant in one fell swoop: ba-da-boom, the battle is won, the pain is gone, and we are ready to take on the world! Wahoo!! Unfortunately, that's just not how it works and for good reason. This is not without exception, but like everything else in life, we learn and grow from the pain and effort, not the quick fix. God is not a genie. We can't just rub on the Bible and say a quick "Oh, Jesus, fix it!" prayer and expect that it will all be taken care of as we snap our fingers and run out the door. God wants a relationship with us, and that means time. The primary reason for our trials is to draw us into spending time with

God's Word Heals

our Lord. And, yes, I know you're busy, but if the God of the universe isn't too busy for you, and He promises to hear and answer, fight for, and deliver you, fulfill His purpose and redeem your life, you have everything to gain by sinking into Him and cherishing His heart for you.

> He himself bore our sins in his body on the tree, that we might die to sin and live to righteousness. By his wounds, you have been healed.
> —1 Peter 2:24

Did you catch that last part? *You have been healed. Have been.* Past. Already done. Your emotions, your heart, your sadness, your pain—it's already healed. Jesus did that on the cross. If you believe that Jesus is the Son of God, that He died on the cross to forgive your sins, was raised again, and lives at the right hand of God Almighty, if you confess Him as your Savior and Lord, then you are *already healed* in Jesus' name! We don't need to keep asking for the healing, we need to thank Him for already healing us. We can walk in faith knowing that even if we don't feel it right this minute, even though it may take more time spent in His presence before we see and feel the evidence, the healing is already bought and paid for with His precious blood.

Now, please do not read a guilt trip into this if you have struggled here. Remember the two-and-a-half years of counseling I had? It takes time, and there are so many layers that need to be healed.

One of the hardest things for me to get past during this time was that no matter how hurt I was, no matter how bad the threats and lies became, my battered heart could not seem to let go and stop caring about what he thought of me. One day, at the advice of a dear friend who had been in my shoes, I sat on my couch and said, "Okay, God, I cannot go on like this anymore. You have GOT to help me STOP loving him. You gave me this love for him as my husband, and now I need for you to take it away from me. And I'm not getting up from this spot until it's gone." Now, I'm not in the habit of demanding things from God, and I don't recommend it, but at this moment I was in such agony, and I knew that it was not God's desire that I continue this emotional bondage to a man who had so deeply betrayed me on so many levels.

I think I sat there for maybe twenty minutes or so, in tears and in prayer, before I felt anything move. Suddenly I felt this warm stirring in my chest, followed by a sharp gasp as it took my breath, and finally a calm and completely overwhelming peace. My tears began flowing again as I realized what had happened. God had answered me right then and there, and I have never been the same. God did what only He can do, and He literally obliterated that emotional connection that had been so painfully barring me from moving forward.

I still struggle with some emotional and verbal triggers now and then, but I remind myself—and the enemy—that I am healed in Jesus's name, because He said so, and I believe Him. The promise of healing is worth holding on to. Faith is believing that what we can't see is still true because God says it is true. Believe it till you see it. Thank Him for it while you wait. Put on the praise music, make a journal of all He has already done that you are grateful for, then rest in Him and in the knowledge that He is faithful. He loves to hear our praise and thanks, and He loves to see our faith in action as we walk with our head held high *knowing* that He *will* do what He says He will do. It's who He is. He can't help it.

Here are a few more of my favorite verses of Scripture. Let them sink into your spirit and encourage your heart.

> The eyes of the Lord are on the righteous, and His ears are open to their cry for help.
> — Psalm 34:15 (CSB)

> Those who look to Him are radiant with joy; their faces will never be ashamed.
> — Psalm 34:5 (CSB)

> The Lord your God is among you,
> a warrior who saves.
>
> He will rejoice over you with gladness.
>
> He will be quiet in his love.

He will delight in you with singing.

— Zephaniah 3:17 (CSB)

I encourage you to search His Word for verses that touch your heart. The Bible is living and active, and He will lead you to His words for you, if you will ask and search. Some great Bible apps and websites are available where you can search by subject or even by how you're feeling. Use them. Ask friends for Scriptures that have helped them in tough situations. (This is where social media can actually be quite helpful.) Then write them out and post them all over your home so that every time you pass by those words you will be reminded of His faithfulness, His love for you, His attentiveness to your cry, and His promise to be everything you need.

— 4 —

My Posse

> My beloved friends, let us continue to love
> each other since love comes from God. . . .
> My dear, dear friends, if God loved us like this,
> we certainly ought to love each other.
>
> —1 John 4:7, 11 (MSG)

I'm so thankful for my posse. My *people*, my *crew*, my *tribe*—whatever term you want to use—it's the people who surround us that matter most.

My parents and my sister and brother-in-law all live within thirty minutes of me, and they have always been a faithful, strong, and godly support. Like any family, we have had our differences over the years, but we always come back to the fact that we love each other and we love Jesus, and that is all that matters in the end.

I confided in my parents and in my sister, Kristi, always—though I admit I left out details I was too embarrassed to share—and when my world came crashing down around me, they were there. No matter what I needed, they were there. Kristi would come and spend time with me and the boys, or just me sometimes, as often as she could. When we knew there would be no reconciliation, my mid-kid suggested that I completely redecorate my bedroom. He said, "Make it girly, Mom. Make it *your* room." So my sister came and helped me paint my bedroom and bathroom the most beautiful ocean blue so it would truly feel like a place of refuge. I loved that room. I got a new chandelier that added to the girly feel, and again Kristi helped me with making new shades for my bedroom, kitchen, and dining room windows. We talked often on the phone—still do—and she checked in on me regularly during those long and painful months. We are just about as opposite as you can be, and yet we have our love for Jesus and our love for each other and our families that keeps us strong. I love that we are getting closer all the time and wish we hadn't waited so long.

My mom and I have always been close, and I loved the extra time we spent together when my babies were really babies. Mine are her only grandchildren, so when my oldest was born there was no way she was missing out on anything! I stayed home with all my boys, so we had a lot of time to hang out with Grandma, and I'm so grateful my boys have had that time as well. My parents are the ones who are at every sporting event (and with three boys, that's a lot of games over the years), every spelling bee, band concert, theatrical play, awards ceremony, and so on. If it involves their grandboys, they'll be there.

When my oldest was about two, he started spending the night at Grandma and Grandpa's house. It's been such a special treat for them to go one at a time, as the boys loved getting special attention, and my parents enjoyed that they were a bit calmer on their own than with a brother or two. My boys are so close to them even now that, even in their later teen years, they still love to spend the night, playing cards and soaking up the time with Grandma and Grandpa. I love that they have that multigenerational relationship to learn from and treasure. It was also a place of refuge and peace at a very tumultuous time in their lives, and I am so grateful we were all able to escape to such a wonderful place.

As I've said, the time between the separation taking place and the divorce being finalized was just shy of two years. I remember feeling so embarrassed and ashamed when I told my dad that my marriage was over. He comes from a long line of faithful believers, and I am the only one on his side of the family who has been divorced. The guilt was almost unbearable, and the idea that I had disappointed him was crushing, but once again, my daddy emerged as my hero. He was so compassionate and loving and totally accepting of me as he vowed to do whatever he could to help and support me and my boys.

I remember one day in particular. I was having an especially difficult, emotionally turbulent time. I had been unable to focus on work that day and had finally given up and was lying on the couch, curled up in a ball, tears rolling down my cheeks and soaking the pillow. The doorbell rang, and I didn't move. It rang again, so I got up and peeked out the window to see my sweet daddy standing there. I opened the door and nearly fell into his arms. He had been praying for me and felt like God just said that he needed to come and see me right away. So he did. I love that about him—he listens when God talks to him. He doesn't question it; he just goes.

We sat and talked for about thirty minutes. He prayed with me, and then he drove thirty minutes back home. That changed my entire day and obviously had an impact far beyond that day, since I'm telling you about it as the tears of gratitude, sorrow, and hope well up in me again, even as I write. I went from feeling despondent and defeated to feeling loved and revitalized in that short time, all because my dad listened to the gentle voice of God

My Posse

and obeyed. His willingness to act made all the difference.

My parents are ninety and eighty-three now, and I am thankful every day for the love and wisdom they have poured into my boys and me over the years. They sit together every morning and pray over my boys and me as well as many others, both family and friends, and I see and feel the difference it makes every day. What a legacy they will leave.

I have amazing friends and extended family who are also loving, gracious, and supportive and a church family that walked prayerfully and faithfully with my boys and me through those dark days. There were Sunday mornings that every ounce of my grief must surely have been evident on my face, and someone—sometimes a close friend, sometimes a woman I barely knew—would stop me and wrap me up in her arms and just cry with me.

One morning during that horrible waiting period, where the threats came often and cut deep, I must have looked like I had tangled with a tiger. As I walked from my seat in the second row in the front of the church where I always sat—and still do—a sweet woman who I was in Bible study with got up out of her seat and enveloped me in the most incredible hug I had probably ever experienced. I didn't say a word, and neither did she, but we stood there clinging to each other for dear life, as we cried with an intensity that threatened to consume us both. I have no idea how long we stood there as the rest of the congregation continued to worship around us, but I can tell you that those were some of the most healing tears I cried, the ones accompanied by those of a friend.

I could not possibly have made it through those two excruciating years—or the previous fifteen—without all those who surrounded me in person and in prayer, those who live close by and those in other parts of the country. Having friends and family who stand with you are a beautiful gift from our loving God.

I surrounded myself with people who would lift us up, both in prayer and encouragement. It made an enormous difference.

My Posse

Words are powerful.

Words can tear us down.

Words can also elevate us.

When someone speaks kindness to our hurting soul, it matters. When someone takes the time to *see* us and speak God's truth into our heart, it changes the outlook of the moment and paves the way for us to visualize ourselves in a new light. Sometimes we must dig for our own truth. We have to look deep inside, back to a time where we were free to be ourselves without fear of rejection or criticism, and ask some introspective questions like *Who was I? Was I happy? Was I kind? Did I dance? Did I laugh? What made me laugh? What did I love doing? Who knows that part of me?*

When I thought about a time I was truly happy and the people who were around me then, I was taken back to my college days at Kansas State University. I had lived with a couple of girls over the summer one year, and Stacey and I became instant friends. That friendship has remained strong to this day. As I was attempting to remember the real me, I called Stacey and asked her what she remembered about me, about who I had been some twenty-two years earlier. She gave me the words I needed to form an image in my mind about who I was and who I wanted to be again. She reminded me that I was fun and carefree, that I loved to laugh and dance around the house. She reminded me that I was trusting and strove to see the best in those around me, that I could simplify things down to see the bottom line—the heart of the issue—and that I am not simpleminded but that God has blessed me with His wisdom to share with others. Because she took the time to see me, I was able to see myself again—the true, free woman God created me to be—and I set that as a goal for the woman I would endeavor to become again. The truth shifted my entire path.

Those who knew me before I began to shrink into that weak, sad, hurt, unhappy girl were so helpful in reminding me of my true self. They have walked with me as I continue to work hard to reconnect with this woman that God has created—this fun, happy, smart, capable, loving, free daughter of the King. It is a journey, to be sure, but one I gladly travel as I continue to take steps toward the woman God had in mind when He created me. I am eternally grateful for each one who walks this life with me.

> *Having people around us who speak affirmation to us on a regular basis is crucial, but know this: YOU ARE STRONGER THAN YOU THINK YOU ARE. You CAN do this hard thing. I've been there. I believe in you.*
>
> *Think back to a time when you felt happy and free to be yourself, with no concern of rejection. Who were you with? What were you doing? What specific feelings are associated with that time and those people? How can you plot steps to get that joy back? Be sure to recognize that the joy comes from the Father. Make worship a regular part of your day. Just reading through the book of Psalms will put you on the path to*

praise. One of my favorites is Psalm 71:14: "But I will hope continually and will praise you yet more and more." Praise Him for what He has done, what He is doing, and what He will do in your future. He's got it all in His loving, gracious, and redemptive hands.

— 5 —

Our Furry Miracle

> *Do not be anxious about anything, but in every situation, by prayer and petition, with thanksgiving, present your requests to God. And the peace of God, which transcends all understanding, will guard your hearts and your minds in Christ Jesus. . . . And my God will meet all your needs according to the riches of his glory in Christ Jesus.*
> *– Philippians 4:6-7, 19 (NIV)*

One of my favorite things about God is that He knows what I need without my having to figure it out and put it into words. He is always working ahead, orchestrating everything exactly on point, to ensure that it comes along at precisely the right moment, in ways and places that often surprise. I don't know about you, but knowing and believing this and resting peacefully in its truth are often disconnected for me. Come on, be honest; I know it's not just me. We try so hard to wait patiently, don't we? Yet, far too often we find ourselves in a panic because we tend to have an insatiable need to have some semblance of control over what goes on in our lives. What I love, though, is that our Heavenly Father knows us so well and loves us so much that He intervenes anyway and comes through for us over and over. He is faithful even when we are not.

I love how God takes care of His kids, and every time I allow Him to be sovereign, my faith is made stronger as I see Him working on my behalf. One particular instance in the fall of 2014 was no exception.

My friend Micah loves dogs—and bunnies, and guinea pigs, and . . . well, you get the idea. She decided that I needed one—a dog, that is. I had been separated for a few months, and the boys had started spending every other weekend with their dad. The house seemed so big and so quiet when they were gone, and I had a lot of time to feel very alone. All my friends are married, most with kids at home, and weekends are their family time. I was happy to have some downtime (many weekends I didn't even leave the house), which gave me time to binge watch Netflix or the Hallmark Channel, but still I was at times almost overcome with the reality of my aloneness, predominantly at night.

Being the intuitive friend that she is, Micah started sending me pictures of dogs she found online—mostly littles like Libby, her sweet Brussels griffon—who needed a home. I kept telling her I didn't need anything else to take care of, but after a while I started thinking that it would be nice to have a bigger dog for a sense of protection, and my boys really missed our schnauzer that had passed the summer before.

So I began the search on a local classified ad website, and after several days of compelled hovering, I found our perfect pup: a beautiful Lab/Rottweiler mix with the sweetest golden brown droopy eyes you've ever seen. According to the ad, he was three years old, house-trained (no way was I potty training a dog with everything else going on), not destructive, great with kids and other dogs, and was very much a lapdog. A military couple had adopted him a few weeks prior but then found out they were being transferred and could not take him along, so they were looking to re-home their sweet pup.

After thinking it over that evening, I emailed the owner to see if the dog was still available for re-homing. Sadly, he was not; he had gone with a single woman the day before. I was so disappointed that I couldn't even look for another dog for a couple of weeks, and then there just weren't any dogs available that tugged at my heart like he had.

It was about three weeks after he had been adopted that I got an email. Apparently, the woman who had initially beat me to the punch had decided she didn't really have enough time for him, so she'd brought him back. The couple had already moved, and the dog was with a family member for the time being, but she was not able to keep him long term, so I had another chance. I, of course, responded to the email immediately with an impassioned "We'll take him!!" proclamation, which was met with gratitude and relief from his previous owner. She was grateful that he would be loved and happy in his new home, and I can't even explain to you how excited I was!

The boys and I went to meet him the next day, instantly fell head over heels in love, and brought home our adorable seventy-pound furry friend. His name is Franklin, and he's perfect! He has the softest and shiniest black fur, a white stripe down his chest, and beautiful brown feet marked by matching black spots on the front two. He has little dots of brown on his very expressive eyebrows and a patch of brown under his chin.

He's a total Mama's boy and wants to be wherever I am all the time. And he *loves* to snuggle. He became my confidant and my shoulder to cry on. He makes me laugh and gets me outside to get some sunshine and exercise. He has *the best* facial expressions and keeps us laughing with his hilarious antics. He talks to us all the time and wags his tail so hard that he whacks himself in the face (I swear he has hinges in his sides!). Best. Dog. Ever.

There are many comical stories about Franklin, but I must share one of my favorites with you. (If you're not a dog lover, please bear with me.) Our backyard was enclosed by a wood privacy fence about six feet high. We hadn't had a dog in over a year, so the bunnies and squirrels were under the impression that they were the rightful owners of the yard and took every opportunity to make themselves at home. A couple of days after we brought Franklin home, I looked out to see two squirrels chasing each other along the top of the fence at the back of the yard—down the length one way and then back again, having an absolute ball. Franklin apparently caught sight of this as well and wanted to join in the fun. I nearly tripped over him as we jockeyed for position at the door but was finally able to reach the handle and let him out. Just as I caught my balance, I nearly lost it again while laughing hysterically as he deer-hopped across the yard, jumped as high as he could, and smacked one of the squirrels square in the side with his shiny black nose! That squirrel went flying off the top of the fence, legs splayed, eyes wide, mouth gaping, and as he flew, the boys and I laughed till our sides ached. We've told that story many times, but even as I write it again, I am in tears! It was seriously one of the funniest things I have ever seen. (I wish I had a video; I would put a link right here.)

Our sweet Franklin has been a source of joy from the minute we saw him. God knew we needed him as much as he needed us. He was between homes with no place to go, and we became his fifth and forever home, giving him the attention, love, and care he needed. We were all a bit lost and a bit lonely in our state of grief and confusion, and he became that unconditional love, loyalty, and unabashed joy that we craved. Franklin is and was our furry gift, straight from our faithful and all-providing God.

God uses so many things to show His love for us in tangible ways. One of my favorite ways is when He works through our friends. Do *not* underestimate the power of this incredible gift! I have been abundantly blessed by those who have stepped out as they were prompted to call, visit, bring a meal, give a hug, send a card, or do a myriad of other small gestures that were monumental blessings at a time when we were all struggling in ways we couldn't understand or even verbalize at the time. I am grateful beyond words.

> *If you're feeling lost, confused, lonely, sad, or alone, ask God to show you His love through those around you. It may even be someone at the grocery store who gives you a compliment or a smile. Don't take anything for granted, but watch for God to show up in others, and then be sure to thank Him for His faithfulness and love. Watch closely and expectantly; you may be surprised where it comes from.*
>
> *If you have a friend, co-worker, neighbor, or family member who you know is in a difficult situation or is walking through grief, please do NOT underestimate your ability to be a blessing. God has planted you there.*

Don't miss an opportunity to walk alongside a fellow sojourner. You may never know the difference you have made or how far-reaching the impact, but you can know that God will use it and multiply it, and you will also be blessed as you minister to others.

— 6 —

Oh, My Heart

> *Trust in the Lord, and do good;*
> *so you will live in the land, and enjoy security.*
> *Take delight in the Lord,*
> *and he will give you the desires of your heart.*
> *Commit your way to the Lord;*
> *trust in him, and he will act.*
> *He will make your vindication shine like the light,*
> *and the justice of your cause like the noonday.*
> *– Psalm 37:3-6 (NRSV)*

Two years, six months, and nineteen days after he walked out on me, and life as I had known it was over, I took a risk that changed my life yet again.

Oh, My Heart

I went on a date.

I had not yet met but had talked with a man named Don on the phone for twenty minutes or so one Sunday. On Thursday, we met for lunch. I had been on a few dates that summer, but this one felt different from the beginning. I was full of butterflies and giggles, which is not a good look when you're forty-eight years old. I'm supposed to be all put together and professional, right? Well, whatever that means to most people, that's not at all who I am. I giggle. A lot. I get tickled about the silliest things, some of which don't even make a lick of sense. I've been ridiculed for it—some people have no appreciation for joy—but I've also been told it's one of the things that makes me approachable and friendly and fun. I could only hope that either I wouldn't be uncontrollably giddy for the entire meal or that he would be extraordinarily understanding.

I remember the song that was playing on the radio as I drove to the restaurant. It was Hawk Nelson's "Live Like You're Loved." I love Christian music (it's pretty much all I listen to, especially in my car), and I have been so blessed by so many songs over my lifetime. This one is no exception, and I just have to share a bit of it with you and encourage you to look it up and listen to it for yourself. It was undoubtedly God-inspired for exactly that moment.

This perfection you're chasing
Is just energy wasted
'Cause He loves you like you are!

So go ahead and live like you're loved
It's okay to act like you've been set free
His love has made you more than enough
So go ahead and be who He made you to be

And live like you're loved
live like you're loved
live like you're loved
live like you're loved

And live like you know you're valuable
Like you know the one that holds your soul
'Cause mercy has called you by your name
Don't be afraid to live in that grace

(Atlantis Underwater Music (SESAC) / FairTrade Tunes (SESAC) / (admin at EssentialMusicPublishing.com. All rights reserved. Used by permission.)

Did you just get chills too?! I know I did, then and now. You gotta love God's sense of timing.

Anyway, before I got out of the car, I let the song finish and just sat back, smiled, and said, "Good one, God. You got me." I think I was still laughing when I walked in the door. I mean, how awesome is it that God puts the words in my head I need to hear, the assurance and reminder that *HE* loves me and that I am valuable and set free? What an awesome God.

I walked into the restaurant, and the hostess showed me to the table where he was sitting. Right away I felt a peace wash over me. He was the perfect gentleman and made me feel so comfortable and relaxed. We chatted easily while waiting for our lunch to arrive and continued in conversation as we ate, exploring the subjects of our kiddos (my three and his three), our jobs, hobbies, political views, and religious beliefs—not easy things to navigate but necessary to know up front, in my opinion.

We had finished our meal, and our conversation was still going strong as he asked if I'd like dessert. I declined, but he went ahead and ordered a dessert to go. He explained that he had a couple of assistants in his office who enjoyed dessert, as he did, but none of them wanted more than a bite or two. So, whenever he went out to lunch, he would get a dessert to go for them to share.

Now, I don't know about you, but that was so huge to me. Here's a man who is on a date and is still able to think of his staff to the point of ordering a dessert for them, not concerned with what I would think, but just being true to who he is. I remember telling a friend about how impressed I was with his selfless generosity and thoughtfulness, and she commented that it was a pretty risky move on his part, that most women would have been offended by his actions, since two of the assistants are women. It never occurred to me to be offended. I just appreciated the thoughtfulness.

We talked a few more minutes before he glanced at his phone to check the time. He nearly leaped from the booth and ran out the door as he realized that he had an appointment and was cutting it very close. He did wait for me to get up and walked with me outside, but I was very aware that I needed to hustle if I didn't want to get run over. LOL. He said he'd had a great time and enjoyed meeting me and would call me later. I texted him a couple of hours later to thank him again for lunch and to let him know that I had enjoyed our time.

We went out to dinner and a movie the following weekend, then another lunch the week after. He had a business trip the week after that, and I offered to take him to the airport and pick him up a couple of days later when he arrived back home. Something sort of magical happened while he was gone—we both felt it. I think we texted more during that three-day trip than we had in the entire three weeks prior. I picked him up from the airport, and the rest, as they say, is history.

That was two and a half years ago, as I am writing. We had dated for just over nine months when he proposed, and we were married twenty-four days later. Yes, I said *days*. I have never felt so safe in all my life as I feel when I am with this wonderful man whose name I now share. He is loving and kind, gentle and supportive, caring and protective. We have never fought. He does not ever raise his voice. Not ever. He is the complete opposite of what I knew and the epitome of the husband I had dreamed of as a young girl. I am truly able to be myself without fear of rejection or even criticism from him. He wholly and completely loves me as I am, even when I feel silly and dance around like a goofball.

We were married at the church my boys and I had attended for nearly eleven years and that Don had started attending several months earlier. Our wonderful Pastor Nathan, who had walked through the last months of my first marriage and the twenty-two months of the separation and divorce, now had a front-row seat to God's redemptive blessing for me and for my boys, as he officiated our wedding.

It was a perfect day in August, which is typically hot and so humid it takes your breath away, but our wedding day was a clear, sunny 77 degrees with a light breeze. We were able to take pictures outside without so much as breaking a sweat at two o'clock in the afternoon! (The following year, on our first anniversary, it was 92 degrees. I'm just saying.) It was a perfect ceremony too. Just the two of us and our six kids, our pastor, and a photographer. It was a wonderfully simple blending of eight people brought together by the grace and providence of the Almighty. My heart bursts all over again just thinking about it.

I know that not every story turns out this way, but this is my story, and this is the evidence I have that God has worked everything for good, as I trusted Him. His redeeming grace is overwhelming to me, and I am grateful beyond words for Don's example to my boys of what it looks like to love a woman in a healthy and God-honoring way, to work and live generously, and to treat all people with dignity and respect.

Our heavenly Father knows how to give good gifts to His children. He has an abundance of grace and redemption and favor for me and for you. I don't know what that looks like for you, but I know it's good. I know that if you trust and follow Jesus with your whole heart, He has only good for you. Are you trusting Him? Are you waiting on Him? I challenge you to let Him be your everything. Make Him the priority and follow Him. Don't jump ahead. Don't go for what you want and ask Him to bless it and make it good; wait on His timing and be willing to receive the gifts He has for you. He knows best what you need. He loves you more than you know. Trust Him.

— 7 —

It's All Jesus

> You, Lord, are all I have,
> and you give me all I need;
> my future is in your hands.
> How wonderful are your gifts to me;
> how good they are!
> – Psalm 16:5–6 (GNT)

So be truly glad. There is wonderful joy ahead, even though you must endure many trials for a little while. These trials will show that your faith is genuine. It is being tested as fire tests and purifies gold—though your faith is far more precious than mere gold. So when your faith remains strong through many trials, it will bring you much praise and glory and honor on the day when Jesus Christ is revealed to the whole world.

You love him even though you have never seen him. Though you do not see him now, you trust him; and you rejoice with a glorious, inexpressible joy. The reward for trusting him will be the salvation of your souls.
– 1 Peter 1:6–9 (NLT)

*Lord, You are my portion and my cup of blessing;
You hold my future.
The boundary lines have fallen for me
in pleasant places;
indeed, I have a beautiful inheritance.*
– Psalm 16:5–6 (HCSB)

I have a dear friend named Cathy, and when someone compliments her (which is quite often, she's that amazing!), she responds with "Thank you; it's all Jesus." I love that about Cathy. She is an accomplished professional, a mom, grandmother and friend, loved by all who truly know her as a kind and selfless encourager and builder of others. She knows which side her toast is buttered on, and she knows the hand who gives the bread and spreads the butter. She works diligently and truly deserves the accolades, but she knows that all of it—the talents and abilities, the opportunities, the connections—is because of God's grace and provision. I love that she knows the importance of recognizing where it all comes from. She doesn't just thank Him privately, but she truly gives Him the glory by recognizing Him out loud to anyone who will listen. It's all Jesus. When life is perfect and when it's not, she gives Him the glory. Cathy's life hasn't all been easy—she's got a beautiful redemption story—but she knows what matters, and she knows who has walked with her and who has held her up. *It's all Jesus.* I love that she knows that. I love that she shares that truth with those of us in her world.

I often find myself trying to be so strong, trying to prove that I'm not broken, trying to show somebody that I didn't let abuse win—that divorce did not destroy me, that I am a great mom even though I've done it mostly by myself, that I am now a caring, loving wife to the most amazingly wonderful, loving, generous, patient, kind man who is truly the perfect fit for me and the wonderful, godly example for my boys that I prayed for many times over.

Still, too many times I find myself forgetting the one thing that matters above all: *it's all Jesus.* Had it not been for *His* grace, *His* mercy, *His* strength, *His* story, *I* would still be broken, *I* would still be lost, *I* would surely have been destroyed. I have not parented these boys alone because God is the perfect Father and He parents them with me, along with my family, dedicated friends, and our church family. I would not have found my perfect-for-me husband without God's provision and His leading us to each other. I am who I am, I am where I am, and I have the strength I have ONLY because of Jesus. *It's. All. Jesus.* When life is easy and when it's hard—because, as we all know, sometimes life *is* HARD—He is still the one in control. He's still the one holding my hand and my heart. He's still the one who holds my kiddos, their today and their tomorrows, their friends, where they go to college and the decisions they will make there, their future mates and families, all of it. He's still the one who holds my future. Come what may, He is still my solid rock, the one I stand on, the one I lean on, the one I cling to.

We each have our own story. My story is not just like anyone else's, and neither is yours, but that doesn't mean we can't stand together or don't understand each other's pain and heartache. We all have hard things happen, sometimes even earth-shattering, devastating things, but we are not defined by those things that happen to us. We are defined by what we do with those things, how we react, where we run, whether we toss our faith off a cliff or come through the fire with a stronger, more intimate faith than we've ever known before. That is what defines us. We all have hard things. What will you choose to do with them? Will you stay a victim and let the other person, the circumstance, the battle defeat you and continue to steal more of your life from you? Or will you get up, take the hand of Jesus, and determine to walk through the fire with your head held high? You can do this hard thing, and it is worth doing well. Make this journey about hope rather than despair. Overcome those limiting beliefs by allowing Christ to be your strength and the voice you choose to listen to. He says you are loved with an everlasting (endless, timeless, indestructible, constant) love. He says you are strong when *He* is your strength. He says you belong because you are His.

> Israel, the Lord who created you says,
>> "Do not be afraid—I will save you.
>> I have called you by name—you are mine.
>> When you pass through deep waters,
>> I will be with you;
>> your troubles will not overwhelm you.
>> When you pass through fire,
>> you will not be burned;
>> the hard trials that come will not hurt you.
>> For I am the Lord your God,
>> the holy God of Israel, who saves you."
>
> – Isaiah 43:1–3 (GNT)

Read that again. You *know* whose you are. *You are His.* He will save you and has called you by *name*. Not "Hey you." Not any of the other hurtful, destructive things that someone else has called you. Not "too fat to love," not "too stupid to have a conversation with," not "disgusting" or "terrible at everything." He calls you by name. He keeps you afloat in the rushing water. He shields you from the flames, smoke, and heat of the fire. He IS "the Lord your God, the Holy One of Israel, your Savior." You *know* He will never leave you or turn His back on you. You *know* you are never alone, not even for an instant. Whether you feel it in the moment or not, read it till you believe it.

> *God did not create you to live your life as a victim. He did not create you to live in fear and defeat. He created you for more. He created you to thrive! If you can't do it on your own, GOOD FOR YOU!! You were never meant to. Grab the hand of God and say, "Okay, I'm ready. I'm ready for more. I'm ready to live out the beautiful inheritance you have given me. I'm ready to step out and be everything you dreamed for me to be when you created me and set me apart for*

your glory. Lead me, Jesus. Lead me, Jesus. For your glory." Now relax, breathe Him in deep, and follow Him to your abundant future.

It is Jesus who fills me with his "inexpressible joy." It is Jesus who reminds me that He made me for more than I can imagine. It is Jesus who calls me daily to follow Him to the abundant life that He has already built just for me. It's Jesus. It's all Jesus. I owe Him everything.

About the Author

Cindi Morse is married to Don. She is mom to Jackson, Dawson, and Roman, stepmom to Drew, Adrianna, and Sydney, and dog-mom to Franklin. She enjoys reading, baking, hiking, traveling, spending time on the beach, mani-pedi day, and sweet white wine. She has a passion for working with women as a writing coach and editor to bring their stories of God's grace and redemption to life for the glory and honor of Christ. For more information or to contact Cindi, please visit her website cindimorse.com.

Made in the USA
Coppell, TX
08 March 2021